JOURNEY THROUGH THE MIND OF A POET

Richard I. Harry

Dadielte Production
Moreno Valley, CA

Copyright© 2016 by Richard I. Harry
Moreno Valley, California

All rights reserved. No part of this book may be reproduced or transmitted in any form or by any means, electronic or mechanical, including photocopying, recording, or by an information storage and retrieval system – except by a reviewer who may quote brief passages in a review to be printed in a magazine, newspaper, or on the Web – without permission in writing from the publisher. For information, please contact Dadielte Production, P.O. Box 1266, Moreno Valley, CA 92556-1266.

ISBN-978-0-9799273-8-6

Published and distributed by
Dadielte Production
P.O. Box 1266
Moreno Valley, CA. 92556-1266

First Printing,
Cover design by marcSierre'

Author's Biography

Richard I. Harry a native New Yorker started writing in 1994. He is the recipient of the Poet of the Year Homer Award (1998 and 1999), Prometheus Muse of Fire Trophy (2001) and the Shakespeare Trophy of Excellence (2002).

He is a member of the Riverside Renaissance Writers and Poets of the Inland Empire.

He is the Author of "Windows of the Mind" (2006) published by Publish America. His poems have appeared in "Cherished Poems of the Western World" Published by the Famous Poets Society also in "A Renaissance Decade" an anthology published by Renaissance Press (2002)

He has performed in New York, New York- Chicago, Illinois- Tampa, Miami, Jackson and Orlando, Florida- Oklahoma City, OK.-Phoenix, Arizona- Memphis, Tenn.-Jackson, Mississippi - South Carolina and all over California from San Francisco, LA, San Diego, San Jose, Riverside and San Bernardino to name a few.

Internationally in St. Thomas, U.S. Virgin Islands - Port of Spain, Trinidad and Tobago - London, England - Paris, France - Nagoya, Japan - Bangkok and Pattaya, Thailand

DEDICATION

To D. M. Simpson, who pushed me to the edge and almost forced me to submit my books to a publisher, for the invaluable assistance with correcting grammar and punctuation, and participating in the workshops...and for the many hours spent proofreading my last two books, but most of all for having faith in me.

&

To Stephen Roper who served as my mentor and teacher. We worked side by side honing our performance and writing skills. He helped with the research, critiquing, formatting and helping to run the workshops. Steve constantly challenged and encouraged me to improve my artistic endeavors. Recording the spoken word CDs was his brainchild.

ACKNOWLEDGEMENT

My sincerest thanks to D. M. Simpson for working tirelessly, correcting grammar, punctuation, proof- reading and giving sound advice on content and format...also for having faith and encouraging me to finish this book. Most of all I give thanks to God our Father for the inspiration. I express my deepest gratitude for the excellent help from Anna Christian that made publishing this book possible.

Forward

I was first introduced to Richard Harry and his work at a meeting of the Renaissance Writers and poets of Riverside California and I instantly took delight in the way Richard is able to see things in everyday life that many others will look right past. His ability is to discern the uncommon in the common and the irony and absurdities in our daily lives as in "Tell Me". His work also includes issues sobering as read in "Dead Man Walking" and relevant with "Only in America". I also must mention that Richard has a real knack for comedy as with "In the Fast Lane" where we might just get a peek at ourselves. And what friend would not offer words of caution to another as we see in "Road Signs". His wit and wisdom, to me is a comment on the passing scene of life with an underlying nostalgia for what used to be and he lets us know he is a man deeply rooted in his faith and endorses that life path.

I enjoyed the "global" feel in his travel approach to presenting his work and it made me feel as though I had actually covered a lot of ground and I hadn't even left my chair. What a pleasure to take this trip laid out by Richard Harry and enjoy all the ups and downs as we do in life. I am certain you will find the time well spent as you allow yourself to be carried from place to place.

If in your poetry reading you are looking for precision in discrimination of subtle things and progressive fineness in the elaboration of the beautiful, than in this collection you have found what you have been seeking.

Sharon E. Bingaman, RN

DIRECTORY

Dedication ---5.
Acknowledgement-----------------------------6.
Foreword ---7.
Directory---9.
Welcome--12.
1. Daily Rush ---------------------------------------14.
2. Keys to Life ------------------------------------16.
3. The Conqueror ---------------------------------19.
4. The Ember ----------------------------------- -24.
5. In the Fast Lane ---------------------------26.
6. Found ---28.
7. Road Signs ------------------------------------30.
8. Beloved --35.
9. Amigo—Enemigo ------------------------- -37.
10. Beauty ---------------------------------------40.
11. The Country -------------------------------.43.
12. The River ----------------------------------46.
13. Parking Citation -------------------------49.
14. Dead Man Walking ----------------------51.
15. Social Security -------------------------- 55.
16. Sensei's Way ----------------------------59.
17. Only in America --------------------------63.
18. Bread of Life -----------------------------66.
19. Beware --------------------------------------68.
20. Fellowship ---------------------------------69.
21. The Fountain of Youth ----------------71.

22. Still -- 72.
23. Pillow -------------------------------------- 73.
24. Love's Touch ------------------------------ 75.
25. Reasons --------------------------------- .77.
26. Man ------------------------------------- .80.
27. Carnival -------------------------------- .83.
28. Anger ---------------------------------- .87.
29. Tell Me -------------------------------- .90.
30. Pepper Ball --------------------------- 93.
31. A Lament ------------------------------ 99.
32. Ghetto Boy --------------------------- 103.
33. Borrowed Time ----------------------- 106.
34. Confetti ------------------------------- 106.
35 My Friend ------------------------------ 107.
36. Behind the Mask --------------------- 111.
37. At Your Own Risk ------------------- 115.
38. Experience --------------------------- 117.
39. Don't Ask ----------------------------- 119.
40. Serenade ----------------------------- 119.
41. Cool ----------------------------------- 120.
42. The Vision --------------------------- 123.
43. Valentine by phone ----------------- 126.

44. Truth Not Silence ---------------------------127.
45. A Commitment ----------------------------129.
46. Don't Wait --------------------------------131.
47. Night Lights ------------------------------133.
48. Reflections -------------------------------133.
49. Just an Hour ------------------------------134.
50. Witness-----------------------------------137.
51. Window Seat ------------------------------139.
52. Recognition -------------------------------139.
53. Success ----------------------------------140.
54. Life---------------------------------------142.
55 Thank You---------------------------------143.
55. Sunshine Man----------------------------- 144.
56. A Half a Dozen Steps---------------------146.
57. Mentor -----------------------------------149.

Welcome!

Welcome! Welcome especially to those who took the time to peek through the "Windows of the Mind". but that's another story. Come, right this way...step-up and go all the way to the back of the elevator that is going down to the staging area. (The elevator stops with a jolt, the doors open,) watch your step--we are now entering the Realm of Richard I. Harry, where there is no distinction between yesterday and tomorrow, time or distance. Here today is a blend of emotion, imagination and mystery in a vortex created by God encompassing all of life extending from here to infinity. Let me introduce myself - I'm the "Realm Keeper". I will be your guide as we start our "Journey through the Mind of a Poet".

We will travel the highways and byways of life, learning the meaning of freedom in the country and the frustration of being in prison. This journey will take you to exotic lands, past and present, where you will glimpse the inhumanity of man and his governments. You will also experience that mysterious emotion called love, tempered with religious fervor and humor. Whether in the air or on land, riding or on foot, the purpose is to take away the fear and make some things clear.

Shh! Shh! Quiet listen can you hear it, that's the alarm clock letting us know it's time for our <u>Daily Rush</u>

DAILY RUSH

Each day we start with the alarm clock's ring,
The covers are off the bed with a fling.
We don't even notice or hear the birds sing.

We race to the bathroom where we meet
For a quick relief and shower treat.
Then shave and put powder on our feet
As we gargle after brushing our teeth.

Then as we rush around trying to dress,
Making decisions about which outfit is best.
Wondering why children don't clean up their mess.

Then to the kitchen for some breakfast food,
No conversation for it would be rude,
Talking with your mouth full doesn't set the mood.
While your daughter phones some gangster dude.

Then run to the car, back out of the drive,
So starts the action in our daily beehive,
We're just waking up as at the job we arrive.

We never noticed the color of the sky
Or if there were clouds going by.
The beauty of the flowers that caught the eye.

We continue to buzz around trying,
To make money by working, selling or buying.
In the end wind up complaining and crying.

On the job we never take time to say thanks,
But take time to play practical jokes and pranks.
Like putting hot sauce on our coworker's franks.
And only worry about the money we have in banks.

Now we're caught up in the whirlwind of this Life,
Overwhelmed by duties that cause all the strife.
Turning to someone other than husband or wife.

Slow down and set aside a part of the day,
To be still and hear what our Lord has to say,
To start us on our path, steered the right way,
Walking with God on to Heaven we pray.

Fellow travelers, this is important, now that you're awake don't forget to pick up your keys.

THE KEYS TO LIFE

That we should love one another,
Yes, we should embrace each other
Just as we would a long lost brother.
These are the keys to life.

We should trust one another
And pray for one another.
A better life through Christ to discover.
These are the keys to life.

Should love our neighbor and his wife.
We should bring him relief not strife.
By example show how to lead a Christian life.
These are the keys to life.

To pay our tithes cheerfully you know,
Not as a debt we owe,
But a planting of seeds that'll grow.
These are the keys to life.

We need to read our bibles everyday.
And not just on the Sabbath day,
To keep the influence of Satan away.
These are the keys to life.

Of course you must be aware,
While for each other you do care,
The same beliefs you must share.
These are the keys to life.

If you ever had any doubts,
Being true to your spouse,
Is what marriage is all about.
These are the keys to life.

And while your children you do raise,
Diligently teaching with lessons & praise,
So that the world they may amaze.
These are the keys to life.

To humble yourself on your knees,
Lift your eyes to God and beg please;
Forgive me for all my wrong deeds.
These are the keys to life.

Thank Him for all he's done for thee.
Thank Him for all that you can see.
Thank Him for shedding His blood on Calvary.
These are the keys to life.

Whatever you do make sure it's right.
The only things that count in God's sight
Is what you do for Christ.
These are the keys to life.

There's no position any higher,
That you can ever wish to aspire,
Than living filled with Christ fire.

These are the keys to life.

Today we will travel back in time to Israel on Mount Calvary where we'll take a look at,

THE CONQUERER

Mankind looks upon the Nazarene
As a poor born holy man and prophet.
Who on Mount Calvary became a victim;
Displayed in an unforgettable scene.
Suffering misery and humiliation.
Being whipped and crowned with thorns
Has to be considered mean.
Mankind looks at Him suspended between
Heaven and earth and think Him weak
And mistakenly pity, mourn and scream.

Mankind has been lamenting for ages.
If they were in possession of understanding,
They would be rejoicing over His victory.
Happiness, joy and relief would be the rage.
The Cross would be remembered as the key
Our Savior used to open the door,
His blood the Ink written on the pages,
Of the heavenly "Book of Life."
We should sing praises for His words.
They will guide us through future ages.

Jesus the Nazarene was not weak,
He was strong then and is now.
People don't know the true meaning of strength.
Although Jesus appeared to be meek,
He did not lead a life of fear.
Jesus lived as a leader,
As the Savior that we seek.
Jesus was crucified as a crusader.
He died with heroism that frightened,
The killers and tormentors at His feet.

Jesus was like a raging tempest,
When He toppled their tables and drove,
The money changers from the Temple.
Feared not enemies, persecutors or the rest,
Of His killers and, or tormentors.
He was brave and daring and felt free,
To defy all despots oppressors and pests.
He muted evil and crushed falsehood,
Choked treachery and defeated Satan.
In His whole life never failed a test.

He had power over the wind and sea.
The power to walk on the water,
To change water to wine upon request.
Power to heal both you and me.
He raised the dead with a touch or word.
Jesus had the power to cast out demons.
To make the lame walk and the blind see.
First He feed the multitude fish and bread,
Then gave them His words, (the bread of life).
When angered could with a word wither a tree.

He came to send forth a new Spirit,
With enough power to crumble,
The foundation of any government built,
Upon human bones and skulls and sear it.
Demolish mansions built on the graves
Of the weak, and crush the idols,
Erected on the backs of the poor near it.
Those that build magnificent churches,
And temples among the shacks
Of the poor need to fear it.

Jesus did not come to destroy homes,
To build convents and monasteries on the ruins,
Or persuade strongmen to become monks or priest,
To do nothing all day but pray and moan.
He came to make our bodies His temple,
With the human heart as an inner sanctum,
Where the altar is the soul alone,
Served by the mind as a priest.
So sing in strength the song of conquest,
And the hymn of triumph in your home.

Crucified Jesus thou art on the cross
More glorious and dignified than,
The kings of a thousand empires.
As in the agony of death you toss
Are more powerful than a thousand generals.
Thou art more brave and silent,
With thy suffering regardless of the source.
Before thy lashers more resolute.
Than a mountain made of granite rock.
For with You no one will be lost.

With thy sorrows thou art more joyous than spring,
Thy wreath of thorns more brilliant,
And sublime than the crowns,
Of gold and jewels that adorn all other kings.
The splatters of blood upon thy feet,
Are more resplendent than a necklace,
Of pearls, diamonds and other precious things.
The nails piercing your hands,
Are so much more beautiful,
Than a dozen diamond rings.

Forgive the weak who lament thee today,
For they do not know how,
To lament for themselves.
Please forgive them anyway,
For they do not know thou hast,
Conquered death with death.
Bestowed life upon the dead, I say,
Forgive them for they do not know,
That thy strength still awaits them.
For they do not know everyday is your day.

It's getting dark, everyone gather around the fire,
find a log or rock to sit on and warm your hands as
we watch,

THE EMBER

How important is it to fellowship,
In a local church of your choice,
Take a moment think about this and voice,
What effect it may have on your relationship,

With God and your fellow Christians,
Especially those you haven't seen for awhile,
Who don't have transportation and live over a mile
Away before you make a definite decision.

As I did while looking at the flames in the fireplace;
With the tongs, I carefully took a glowing ember,
Placed it on the hearth and watched, I remember,
It flickered then faded, the heat warming my face.

It wasn't long before it was cold and dead.
After a few more minutes of reflection,
I picked up the cold ember and put it back in
The fire in the same section of the fire bed.

Almost immediately it began to glow again so bold,
With the light & warmth of burning coals around it.
Thinking of the warm fellowship of the church it fit.
Fellowshipping keeps your heart from growing cold.

The Lord helps us see how we need each other
As we travel along the Christian way,
He will keep us growing day by day,
In fellowship with sister and brother.

Before you look at the big picture take that beam out of your eye.

IN THE FAST LANE

Early one spring evening
My wife pulled up to my job in our car.
Upon getting out she started screaming,
About how irresponsible other drivers are.

She said, "as I was coming here in the rain
In the fast lane on the freeway.
I noticed the car in the next lane,
Was swerving across the line this way and that way.

When I pulled even with it
I could see that the driver's face was so close
To the windshield, I almost had a fit;
She was putting mascara on in the mirror.

Suddenly the car veered in my direction so quick
It scared me so, I almost crapped,
And dropped my own lipstick,
Right into the cup of coffee on my lap.

The phone I was holding with my chin
Fell out of the window,
As I swerved to the left right then,
She almost caused an accident and didn't know it."

People have traveled around the world looking for what I've

FOUND

Something no power can demand,
No matter how long they plan.
Something influence cannot acquire,
Whether President, politician or liar.

Or with riches try to purchase,
Really would be such a waste.
Nor can it be erased by time.
To even think it would be a crime.

It cannot be deadened by sorrow,
Remembrance of yesterday, or tomorrow,
The reality of which is so vast,
You realize it's nature at last.

Something that gathers strength with patience,
Even when that doesn't make sense.
Like how it grows in spite of obstacles.
Can't be understood even through spectacles.

Something that warms in the winter,
Even cold weather cannot hinder.
Oh! How it flourishes in the spring,
When everyone wants to do his own thing.

In summer it comes on like a breeze,
That can do nothing but please.
And when it bears fruit in the fall,
I want to shout to one and all,

I FOUND LOVE.

As we continue on our journey be sure to keep an eye out for :

ROAD SIGNS

As you travel in today's world
Searching for that special girl.
As time and events unfurl,
Pay attention to the road signs.

Now if you think she really looks fine,
But find her drinking red, red wine,
Morning, noon and at bedtime.
That's definitely a red light.

Now if she is in bad health,
Marrying her depletes your wealth.
You'll regret the hand you're dealt.
That is a stop sign.

Date a Christian for over a year,
And she still calls you honey or dear,
Never asked for money, then it's clear.
That is a green light.

If she has to fuss and fight
With you almost every night,
She says you can't do anything right.
This is a red light.

If you see when you first meet,
That she has braces on her teeth,
She's sure to make your pockets leak.
This is a stop sign.

Be sure you are both in accord,
Believe in God for your just reward.
She has to be one you can afford.
This is a green light.

While you are being patient and wait,
You find she is always late.
Invites her friends out on your dates.
This is a red light.

If her teeth look like a picket fence,
Anyone with common sense,
Can tell she will be a big expense.
This is a stop sign.

She makes your heart flutter with kiss or glance,
After years it's not sex, still love and romance.
Happily you can take the chance.
This is a green light.

She says she has female problems,
Don't try to think of ways to solve them.
She's definitely not your precious gem.
That is a red light.

While on your date she likes to flirt,
Talks of boyfriends who did her hurt,
And often treats you like dirt.
That is a stop sign.

Now if her love for you is true,
There's nothing she won't do for you.
And if you really love her too.
That is a green light.

Now if by chance she's hooked on coke,
This is surely nobody's joke,
There's no way you'd want to be yoked.
This is a red light.

Now if by chance you discover,
The woman is controlled by her Mother,
You had better run for cover.
This is a stop sign.

When she keeps the laws of Christ,
And continues to do what's right.
You should be able to see the light.
Yes this is a green light.

Cigarettes to her have become a need,
Along with Mexican or Columbian weed,
And with same sex couples she has agreed.
That is a red light.

Now if her place is never clean,
Her breath is in need of Listerine.
She doesn't care about hygiene,
That is a stop sign.

When she promises to raise your children,
To teach the keys of life to them,
Protect them like a Mother hen.
That is a green light.

She tells you she is pregnant maybe,
It could be someone else's baby.
She is not your special lady.
This is a red light.

Finally settled in a cozy nook.
For a candlelight dinner by the brook,
Then she confesses that she can't cook.
This is a stop sign.

She says she'll love you the rest of your life,
Through winter storms, in pain and strife,
This is the woman you want for your wife.
This is a green light.

Now that you know she is heaven sent,
Listen if you have any kind of sense,
You know it's time to get a marriage license
This is a green light

Let me caution those who are not traveling with their mates, although we may see many strange and wonderful things please, don't forget your

BELOVED

As strong as superwoman is my beloved.
I pray for the strength to be her sweetheart.
At last we are united by our love.
I go to her in haste and then depart,
Knowing she is truly a work of art.

Yes, she was stolen from my dreams.
Swiftly I cast the silver of my foam,
Upon the down that guards her wet seams.
We blend in melted brilliance as we roam,
About each other with no thought of home.

I have a thirst only she can quench,
She can soften my heart with her voice,
And subdue my temper with a touch.
One embrace and I have no other choice,
Except to hear the melody of her voice.

As she explains to me the rules of love.
My beloved gives me an earful,
Then prints smooth kisses upon my face.
I press on swift and also fearful,
But she is quiet, patient and thoughtful.

Now her bosom soothes my restlessness,
As we begin again to softly caress.
She smiles moans and then gives a breathless sigh.
I rise and plunge into the depths of happiness,
We soar together, join the stars in success.

In the evening I sing songs of hope,
Softly to my beloved one more time.
Knowing she lifted my drowning soul,
And gave me her strength as she took mine.
Leaving me drunk as with fine red wine.

As we take a well deserved break with the friends we've made on this trip, let us reminisce about our neighbors at home are they,

AMIGO – ENEMIGO
or
(ARE FRIENDS TAKING ADVANTAGE)

When they drop their children at your home
For you to baby sit for an hour or two,
And you have to call them on their cell phone,
The next day to remind them that you,
Still have their Be-Be children.

Is he taking advantage again?
When he borrows your car,
For a month while you are on vacation.
From the airport which is not far,
You call to be picked up.

He tells you to wait with your luggage,
Out front of the baggage claim.
"I'm not paying to park in this day and age,
When I can drive by, Just the same,
I'm only going to pass by once."

Was taking advantage part of his plan?
Now how did you feel the day
You asked him to be your best man?
When he asked, "What does the job pay?"
Was his keeping the rented Tuxedo a scam?

Why would they throw a party?
For you in a downtown bar, just think;
Hired lap dancers, told all to drink hardy.
Everyone knows, you're Christian and don't drink.
So you wind up the designated driver.

Didn't you have a hint or suspicion?
As you were roasted and toasted
And promised tomorrow would be a thrill.
About their Weddings joked and boasted,
Then disappeared when they brought the bill.

Do you wonder when it will stop?
Your grown son borrows your car in June,
A month later you answer the door for a cop,
Who hands you a summons to appear at noon.
Your car was in an accident at school.

Your son admitted he let his son Lamar,
Your grandson drive to his senior prom,
Because he didn't trust him with his new car.
Says he did not mean any harm,
When he gave his son the keys to your car.

Take advantage of a married man?
You come home to find your wife in bed,
With guess who? Your best friend Herman.
Her excuse! "I was just proving what I said,
I told you he was no good."

Now you know who to turn to.
Jesus is the only friend,
Who will love and protect you,
From the beginning to the end.
That he laid down his life for you is true.
&
With Christ you have the advantage.

Ladies and gentlemen, put away the mirrors, fold
your tents and look at the real thing, natural

BEAUTY

Some say beauty is the symbol of nature,
The virgin all of our forefathers worshipped.
Erecting shrines and statues of great stature,
Like goddesses in the mind of one on acid.

My life is sustained by the world of beauty,
Which you will see wherever you rest your eyes.
Hills, rivers, trees and plants both sweet and fruity.
Joy and happiness comes when you realize,

That beauty is nature itself.
And has the awe-inspiring power
To usher the wise to the throne of truth.
A worthy experience if only for an hour.

We as humans fear all things,
Even nature, haven of rest and tranquility.
We fear our own desires and feelings,
And heaven, source of peace and spirituality.

Many of us fear the God of goodness.
Accuse Him of anger and terrible wrath,
Although He's shown love, mercy and forgiveness.
Asks us only to return to the right path.

When you meet beauty you will hear,
Her cry deep within your self, if smart
Will stretch forth your hands in love not fear,
To bring her into the domain of your heart.

It is the combination of joy and sorrow
The unseen that you finally see.
It is the vague you'll understand tomorrow,
Silence heard while sitting under a tree.

Beauty dwells in the holy of holies nestled,
Deep within our very souls.
And extends beyond our star speckled
Earthly imagination, whether young or old.

For beauty is that which attracts
Your soul, body and your mind.
That loves to give, never attacks,
Nor looks for favor of any kind.

Head for the stable to climb aboard the hay wagon for today's tour of

THE COUNTRY

My son return to the country to freedom for all not some,
Where there is no boss to make a demand.
When winter exits with her garments, spring must come,
But only at God's great command.

In the city the joy of one is the sorrow of another.
In the country the frolicsome breeze brings joy,
To those who look to nature as a mother,
Who will nurture man, woman, girl and boy.

Your sorrow in the country will vanish as soon,
As the autumn leaf carried on the back of a brook,
Your heart will be as calm as a lake under the moon,
As upon its infinite beauty you look.

Here there's no need to wait for wine to cure.
Glorious intoxication of the soul is the reward,
Of all who seek it in the bosom of nature,
Not pills or drugs that lead to the hospital ward.

No prejudice, color, or creed, in this region,
Nothing's denied or held back beyond reach.
When the Nightingale sings all's beauty, joy and religion,
The spirit is soothed and the reward is peace.

Here justice grants neither favor nor neglect.
Although plants and trees grow in each other's way,
None here complain or object,
For when the wind blows all will sway.

Justice here is like the snow,
It puts a blanket over all things.
And when the sun appears all will grow,
Their beauty and fragrance will make birds sing.

Nature sees neither the weak nor the strong.
To nature all are alive and all are free.
To nature alone all things belong,
The seed, the leaf, the willow and oak tree.

In the country, man's glory is an empty dream,
Unlike the lilies that were made as cups for dew.
Man's glory will vanish like bubbles in a rocky stream,
While the lilies nature will forever renew.

The running streams sweet nectar will fill,
Both man and animal alike,
And as it broadens and stills,
Reflects the truth of neighbor, self and site.

The throne of love is in the field,
Where love and beauty abide,
Forever in peace and bounty never to yield,
As they live side by side.

For the sea and the fog,
The dew and the mist are all one.
Whether cloudy or clear are the gifts of God,
Along with the moon, stars and the sun.

The country gives no heed to desire,
Nor craves for anything large or small,
And fears only the wildfire.
For God almighty has provided her with all.

Renounce the future and forget the past,
Nature will greet you as one of her own,
Everything that is good will come at last.
For the child of the field is the child of God.

Listen up! Put on your life jackets and stay seated while in the rafts as we challenge

THE RIVER

Looking back the first thing I remember,
My maker placing me on the soft bed
Of a cloud, I grew heavier and fell,
Through along with my brothers we landed,
On a steep hillside and tumbled on down.
At the bottom we gathered for a few
Minutes then began to flow through mountains,
Valleys and plains finally arriving,
At the mouth of a slow muddy river,
That eventually flowed underground.

Filtered through mineral, sand and gravel,
Emerging as a crystal clear river;
Whose refreshing waters sparkle with life,
Plankton, larvae, tadpoles, and fish, givers,
Of life for reptile, animal and man.
By picking up speed I carve a route through,
Canyons, deserts, and forests over falls;
Flowing through dams that supply energy,
Recreation and water, quenching thirst,
Nourishing farmlands doing all I can.

Until I reach the sea my destination.
Mankind, can't you see that our path's the same?
Both, fell, I from the clouds, you from the womb,
Landing in the mud not a cause for shame.
Going underground made me fresh and clean,
As you when baptized in His holy name.
Now filled with life I share it wherever,
I go; we both can use living water,
Create physical and spiritual,
Gardens if we leave behind the past and lean,

On our faith in God to carry us forward,
With hands outstretched toward our final goal,
Listen for the sound of a waterfall,
Although hidden by mist, the God of old,
Can still be heard, in the waterfall's roar,
But only in the silence of the soul,
Will His voice be clear, the power of God,
Can work miracles only when it's used,
Like the fall's power, electricity,
Aren't you aware you can do even more?

If you pause and listen to His commands,
Spread the words of Jesus Christ and nourish,
Those along the path that He will reveal.
Now carve your way with a divine flourish,
His power flows through you to benefit,
Others giving them the energy to,
Continue when you satisfy their thirst,
For water that brings everlasting Life,
And a relationship with Jesus Christ,
Who has the only key that's sure to fit.

Jeep parking... head in only... you will be
responsible for your own,

PARKING CITATION

On the front window stuck under the windshield wiper,
Of a car with an alarm system that goes off whenever,
Anyone approaches within three feet, called a Viper,
Turning it on in a parking lot was not too clever.

Nor was taking up three spaces by parking on an angle,
Directly across the street from the police station.
Actions that were sure to make someone strangle,
Them while verbally abusing them without question.

Attached to the citation was this rather caustic note;
It said, if it were within my power you would receive
Three tickets, and believe me I don't mean it as a joke,
Just the thought of someone like you is hard to conceive.

Because of your empty-headed, inconsiderate, feeble
Attempt at parking you have taken enough room,
For a tractor trailer, the reason to me is inconceivable.
I am giving you this citation and a day filled with gloom.

So that in the future you will think of someone else;
Other than yourself, when you park your car anywhere.
Don't even think about throwing this ticket on a shelf.
We will definitely be watching for you, so beware!

Besides! I really don't like domineering, egotistic,
Or simple minded drivers, knowing you probably
Fit into all of these categories, to be realistic
It's very hard to picture you acting sensibly.

I sign off wishing you an early transmission failure,
On the freeway at four in the afternoon rush hour.
May the fleas of a thousand camels have the pleasure,
Of infesting your armpits and groin from shower
to shower.

With my compliments,
          Sergeant R. E. Tribution

Watch your step as you get off the bus. Don't
complain if your feet hurt just be glad you're not a

DEAD MAN WALKING

Like any journey, starts with a single step,
The first when you heard your sentence in court.
Guilty as charged, a car thief with a rep,
A well known three time loser who got caught.

Who would believe, you did not know the baby
Was in the back seat. The court did not care.
You stole the car to impress a lady.
You abandoned the car and left her there,
The baby died so they gave you the chair.

That's when it all started ulcers and pain,
Six years of being raped, beaten and abused,
By inmates and guards, afraid to complain,
Stomach churning as you wait for the news.

Appeal denied, date of execution_____.
Your heart feels like it is lodged in your throat
Every time the guard's keys clink in your section,
Sweating so much you could start your own moat.
Move away from the bars you know the rote.

Followed by the cry dead man walking here,
As another inmate walks that last mile.
Body doubled in pain you shake in fear.
And the tears begin to flow from eyes while,

Guards stand displaying a sardonic smile.
As they take bets on whether or not he walks,
Or will be carried down that narrow aisle.
He wants to act tough but his body balks,
He's so pale they throw him some smelling salts.

The next day he almost had a heart attack,
When the guards came until he remembered,
Chaplain promised a French dinner in fact,
Had turned his office into a restaurant.

Although the food was exquisitely prepared,
The room looked like a restaurant in town
Complete with aroma. He was so scared,
Everything tasted like it was dark brown.
It's no surprise he could not keep it down.

This torture was his life six years of appeals,
A divorce and two years praying to God,
Brought two stays letting him know God was real.
The death penalty caused all this stress, odd!

No! It's not odd for a man under forty,
In good shape to go from weighing a fit
Two hundred pounds. to one hundred and forty;
Broken in his mind, body and spirit,
When faced with the death penalty, hear it.

The quiet at night is broken as he screams,
Waking himself and others in death row,
Each night he sees the grim reaper in dreams.
How he manages without sleep we don't know.

Like a marathon runner he stumbles,
And then falls as he nears the finish line.
His life flashing before him as he crumbles.
Time seems to crawl; no he is not fine,
As he reaches for Jesus his lifeline.

Dead man walking this time he is the one,
Surrounded by guards front, back and both sides,
Head shaved, pants legs slit, everything's done.
Head held down to hide the fear in his eyes.

Finally he looks up to see a room,
Full of people there to witness his death.
He cries out as he sees the chair and doom.
Passes out while trying to catch his breath.
They laid him down calling his name, Seth, Seth.

As the doc. pronounced him dead a pity,
The phone rang it was answered by the warden.
Another victim of the death penalty,
The governor had issued a full pardon.

On this leg of the journey, your passport will be your social security card.

SOCIAL SECURITY

What is social security?
Some books give it the same definition
As the dictionary gives for society.
A group of human beings bound together
For self-maintenance, preservation and continuity.

Sharing culture and complex social relations,
At home, work and at play.
Throughout the city, state and nation.
Security is a guarantee or assurance they say,
It's the freedom from fear, want and deprivation.

What is social security? The concept:
You pay social security tax into the system
Or when you work they take it out of your check
Along with income taxes, federal, state and city.
It's a wonder, that we have anything left.

And when you get old and lose your fire,
If you get hurt or are disabled,
You become a person no one will hire.
And in order to collect any benefits,
You may be forced to retire.

What is social security? What are the facts?
Is it the same as this thing called FICA?
The federal insurance contributions act.
It looks as if Medicare and food stamps
Have joined Medicaid to make a pact.

What is social security? Is it something to hate?
Is it really a retirement plan?
Or just another one of the taxes they take?
How can it be a survivor's insurance plan?
When they take from every dollar we make.

What is social security? Has it gone sour?
Can you believe it a one-time death benefit?
After working 10 to 35 years, all those hours,
To receive only 255.00 dollars.
That just may be enough to cover the flowers.

What is social security? Are the rumors true?
That we have to wait until we are 65 to 67,
Before they will give any benefits to me or you.
I hear there is not enough for our children,
This to me is nothing new.

What is social security? Does it make sense my dears?
For minorities to try to contribute,
When their life expectancy is only 60 to 65 years.
Or less and widows can't collect until they're 60.
It's enough to bring on the tears.

What is social security? I know it can't be,
Living on $769 dollars a month after earning $20,000.
Or $30,000 and get $1,521 that's with a spouse you see.
And if you work to make ends meet,
They take a $1 for every $2 you make, hear my plea.

What is social security? To me it's knowing
That in this country, we have the freedom
Here to get up every morning,
Think of what you want to do,
And try to do it as soon as you're finished yawning.

Here you can say what you desire
Even if nobody wants you to say it.
You can decide something you'd like to acquire,
For yourself and work to get it.
For me this is social security if you inquire.

What is social security? Is it just being aware?
That the sun will rise in the morning,
Because there is a God who cares.
Not only about the flowers, birds and bees,
But also gave us, life to share.

What is social security? A world to live in,
With mountains, rivers, valleys and plains,
Forest, lakes, islands and oceans, because of sin.
But God was merciful and sent His Son,
To guide those that believe back to Him.

For you and me,
This is "Social Security".

This morning we will board a 747 to Tibet where we'll try to understand

SENSEI'S WAY

Sensei standing in his garden of peace,
Amongst plants he's nurtured with loving care.
Arrayed in black ghee, eye patch to match,
Motionless, unseen yet very aware,
Of each man, insect or animal there.

An architect who mastered the wisdom,
Of the eastern martial arts and healing.
Who shared his knowledge and philosophy
And found harmony in photography.
Still many starlit nights in his garden,

He gazes across the moonlit valley
At the path meandering up the side
Of the mountain, along bare windy heights
Watching shadowy figures as they plod.
A strange procession all throughout the nights.

He hears the fly upon the windowpane,
Canine call of the wild, heard as a child,
Sweet sound of birds after the rain,
But never a sound from those travelers,
Neither soft nor harsh voice could he recall.

As upon their silent way they still trod.
They never turn nor pause or stop to rest,
Like serpents' coil upon coil unending,
Moving steadily onward to the west.
Was this some sort of mysterious test?

A sight he has watched for many myriad moons,
But where they are going of what they seek
As they cross the mountains snow covered peak.
Unseen, beyond the mountain answers lie.
He ponders, as from his eye they vanish.

Yet sometimes in dreams he will pass with them,
Where the heavens touch the crown of the hill,
Shade after shade and shadow moving still,
With them he'll pass across meadow and grass
And up to reach the purple mountainside.

To see before him stretching wide the plain,
Filled with beautiful flowers, shady trees,
And gardens where crickets and drowsy bees,
Join frogs making music in the ear of sleep;
While past the banks sweeps a broad blue river.

Roses dream, swans and water lilies sway,
With the slow rhythm of the bubbling stream,
And in the distance milk white doves fly,
Above the tall gleaming marble towers,
That elicited from his heart a cry.

For where the trees most thick and shady are
Appeared a city, shinning like a star.
White marble residences far and near;
White rose gardens everywhere you peer,
From the river that laves her marble quays.

His cry broke the dream and all that was known,
Now was shattered and lost and overthrown,
Still his heart stirred with the longing to join
Those silent travelers strange procession,
Passing day by day on its westward way.

My heart knows that he found the way to go.
At last to rise and join that steady flow,
To seek within the shinning west the gate,
That happy abode of those that enter,
The city of eternal rest and peace.

We will be landing in the U.S. in a moment. After visiting other countries. It is still hard to understand why some things happen

ONLY IN AMERICA

Only in America do they
Have drive-up ATM machines
With Braille lettering.
When did the blind start driving?

Only in America do drugstores,
Make the sick walk all the way to the back
Of the store to get their prescriptions.
Now can you picture that?

While the healthy people
Can buy their cigarettes,
At the front of the store
While they watch their pets.

Only in America do people
Order double cheeseburgers,
Large fries and a diet coke,
This has to be a joke.

Only in America do banks
Leave both doors open,
While tellers behind glass
Mark each bill that you pass;

To test for authenticity
Then chain the ballpoint
Pens to the counter.
Now that's really a pity.

Only in America do people
Build their new homes over
The garage and then leave cars
Expensive enough for stars,

Parked in the driveway;
And put their useless
Junk in the garage,
No matter how large.

Only in America do we
Buy hot dogs in packages of ten
And buns in packages of eight.
When will they get it straight?

Only in America do we
Use the word "Politics",
To describe our governing
Process, its true meaning.

In Latin "poli" means many
And tics means bloodsucking
Creatures which are parasites
And that description is so right.

Only in mainland America,
Can you go to a Hawaiian
Restaurant and order Chinese food
From a waiter who calls you dude.

Watch two different ball games,
While listening to rock music,
And not see one person of color.
A cause to cry in your Mai-Tai.

Only in America could part
Of an E-mail from my brother
Written by someone or other,
Have ended up in this poem.

It is time to interrupt our journey long enough to taste the

BREAD OF LIFE

A Rabbi taught over 2000 years ago,
That God could have created a plant
That would grow loaves of bread, you know!
When it comes to God we never say can't.

Instead for us He created wheat,
To be cut and ground at the mill;
Then baked in an oven with heat,
Served in loaves for us to get our fill.

Why? So we could be His partners,
In completing the work of creation.
And with Christ we can be the gardeners,
Of our own and others salvation.

Few people truly understand that life
Is a fragile bargain at best,
At times we have to deal with strife,
But so do all the rest.

We just have to remember,
Life is rescindable at any time,
By that other party member.
And live our lives accordingly all the time.

No life ever grows great,
Until it is focused on Christ,
Free from all forms of hate,
And channeled to do what is right.

Dedicated to spreading God's word
Throughout this wicked globe.
Discipline ourselves in spite of what we've heard,
To be worthy to wear a heavenly robe.

At the end of that straight and narrow path,
That leads back to our Creator.
To be met with love not wrath,
By Christ our leader and protector.

I want you all to sit back and relax. Leave the worrying to me. As your guide I say

BEWARE

My son beware the demon Stress,
He attacks both body and mind.
Look about you'll find many a witness
To prove his work is never kind.

If allowed will fill your life with clutter,
Sap your strength and dull your skills.
Lack of rest will cause the heart to flutter.
To reverse this effect takes more than pills.

This demon stress works hard all the time
To destroy your mind and health;
Allowing this would be a crime
Leading to his undermining your wealth.

Listen to those who usher in My place.
Carefully manage your time and follow My plan;
You can still …win this race.
Heed this and on holy ground you will stand.

Seek My word and it will be given.
Forget not what you've heard
From those who will utter when bidden.
All the answers are in the Bible …My word

The one thing I want all of you to take home at
the end of this excursion is the meaning of

FELLOWSHIP

Please think of fellowship as a seat
At a round table where no one
Is considered the head or the feet;
Where responsibility is shared by everyone.

Where we practice all for one
And one for all, we declare,
After all is said and done,
It's God's love that we share.

Take notice of the spokes of a wheel,
Each one does its part to support
The whole; they don't make appeals
Or waste time making lengthy reports.

Each depends on the others first and last
To move forward while bearing
And sharing the important task
That we call soul gathering.

As we travel along the road
With the Spirit to guide all who will come
To the same destination with a full load
Of souls bound for God's kingdom

When you travel to paradise, it becomes clear why people search for

THE FOUNTAIN OF YOUTH

In spite of jet travel being the rage,
All this travel was wearing me down.
My boss said, "The more time you spend on jets,
Scientist say the slower you age.
So there is no need for you to frown.
You will feel younger I bet,

When you receive the travel bonus
Check for a substantial amount."
I said," I do not mean to be rude,
But speaking for all of us,
Scientist forgot to take into account,
The quality of airline food.

Although we've traveled through time and space for long distances

STILL

Two hearts still speaking,
With love's sweet tongue,
Two hearts in love,
Will forever stay young.
Two hearts still sharing,
All of love's ecstasy,

Those two hearts still,
Belong to you and I you see.
As we walk together still believing,
Our love is honest not deceiving.
Two hearts will still rejoice,
When I announce my choice,
By saying I Love You "------."

Finally we have arrived at our hotel just in time to lay our heads on the

PILLOW

As I looked upon her resting on my bed,
I noticed the rhythmic rise and fall of her breast.
A thought," what a perfect place for a moment's rest
Came to me as I laid down my head,

On that soft fragrant cushion
Like a bird nestled in a nest;
Down and feathers up to his chest;
Rocked to sleep by the gentle motion,

Eventually turning over to place my ear
Upon her abdomen to listen to the roar,
Did I say roar! No it was much more.
In time I was able to hear.

What seemed like the musical notes
That you hear as you browse through,
The wilderness there is always something new
To hear and feel like the rise and fall of a boat

Sailing on a meandering river,
Flowing gently toward that place
That guarantees the continuation of the race.
Where of my very essence I will give her.

I seem to melt right into her deep,
Until there is no longer a me.
As we share what has become ecstasy.
A feeling I long to forever keep.

But alas no matter how tall my tree
It will fall and plunge over the waterfall
To crash with sounds loud like a thunder ball,
Setting our pent-up emotions free.

I will continue to give and she to receive.
As we work together to plant a seed.
We understand that this is a universal need,
That only those in love truly believe.

Before you move on to your next destination, be sure to experience

LOVE'S TOUCH

Her touch is as soft as a midsummer breeze
And as light as a windblown feather,
This at first sends cold chills through me
To be quickly replaced by a warm glow.

That accelerates to a burning blaze,
Fueled by a building passion,
Fanned by feelings of love
Awakened by the touch of a hand.

That caresses my cheeks and gently
Travels down my body in slow motion,
Stopping for a moment to embrace,
One breast and then the other.

Then continues its slow progress
Massaging its way along my spine;
To its next destination those other
Cheeks patiently waiting to be kneaded.

As the lips and tongue are introduced,
While performing a slow sensual dance,
Soon the tongue abandons the lips
For a rendezvous with the ear and neck.

Meanwhile the hands please and squeeze
The hips and thighs as they meticulously
Search for the forest that contains
The legendary staff of life.

Upon discovery will send an urgent
Message to the twin sets of lips and the tongue,
That their quest is finally over
And they can partake of the nectar of life.

Thereby fulfilling and being filled
With ecstasy as they engulf,
And in turn are fully engulfed,
In the process of making love and life.

Ladies and Gentlemen: We are scheduled to attend
a wedding ceremony during our tour. "Telegram!"
Let me open this and find out the

REASONS
(Why the wedding was postponed)

After three months of exercise and stress
And eating Jenny Craig cuisine.
The bride picked up the wedding dress,
Tried it on and promptly split the seams.

They decided there was too much rear exposure,
Since she could not get satisfactory closure.
*

The groom was given a bachelor party
With strippers at a public bar.
He joined the strippers, after drinking Bacardi
And got arrested when he went too far.

From jail he could not budge,
Until after the weekend and he saw the judge.

The day before the wedding you answer the phone,
It's the bride's family saying the bus they rented
For her relatives, broke down 200 miles from home.
And her dad said he wasn't flying and meant it.

Fear of flying was embedded in his heart.
Mom said from him she would not part.

You're decorating the church banquet hall
With streamers of ribbons and lace.
The minister comes in with your check for the ball
Stamped non-sufficient funds on the face.

He says, "I'm sorry I have to ask
You to replace this check with cash."

The groom (served a subpoena at the rehearsal)
To appear in court for his divorce
That called for a quick reversal
To keep the bride from being scorched;

When she found out he was not true
And had two children, too.
*
It was the worst looking bridal party you ever saw
The bride was sporting a black eye
And the best man a broken jaw.
Now if you're wondering why,

At the rehearsal the groom caught them kissing,
Now the best man has some teeth missing.

Everyone told her it would be a disgrace,
That to walk down the aisle pregnant was no joke.
At eight months it was too late to save face.
Half way down the aisle her water broke!

The baby said, he could not wait
You'll have to set another date.
*
To avoid adding reasons to this list,
Follow Christ's word, live a Christian life.
Worldly life styles are not worth the risk
Of losing the promise of the eternal life,

You will receive when you obey,
God's commandments, and live right.
*
Leave the darkness for His light today,
Knowing he blesses those that walk His way,

Ladies and Gentlemen, we are going to take a step back, back in time to the beginning and take a look at

MAN

He was here from the beginning,
At the worlds end, will be here still
Because of his sinning
There's no end to his grief, as he pays his bill.

He roamed the infinite sky,
Soared high in the perfect world.
Sailed the seas and knows not why.
Some can't decide whether they're boy or girl.
Here he's a prisoner of logic and measure.

He heard the teaching of Confucius,
He listened to Brahma's wisdom.
Buddha said seek peace do not fuss.
All know there is no Magic Kingdom.
Yet here exists in Ignorance.

He was on Sinai when God spoke and Moses read
The Commandments, saw miracles at the Jordan.
He was in Medina when Mohammed visited,
On Calvary when Christ died for all men.
Yet here he is a prisoner of bewilderment.

A witness to the might of Babylon and Rome,
Learned of and saw the glory of Egypt.
Viewed the world's armies and those at Home;
Saw the effect of the chain and the whip.
Taught the weakness and sorrow of these feats.

He conversed with magicians through out time,
Debated with priest of all kinds.
He studied the prophets of Palestine.
Has tried expanding the ability of the mind.
Yet is still seeking the truth.

He gathered wisdom in India and China.
Has heard all that can be heard.
Probed antiquity in Egypt and Arabia;
Knows African wisdom unlike Europe's, is not third.
Yet his heart is deaf and blind.

Has suffered at the hands of despots many.
He suffered slavery after many invasions.
Endured hunger imposed by tyranny,
Experienced natural disasters on many occasions.
Still with some inner power greets each day.

His heart is empty, but his mind is filled.
Has an infant heart but his body is old.
Leaving youth hearts think growing old a thrill;
As he ages it will understand when it's told
The truth, only the return to God will fill his heart.

He was here from the beginning
And at the worlds end, will be here still.
Because of his sinning,
There's no end to his grief, as he pays his bill.

Be sure to take your boarding pass and your passport with you when you leave the ship in Trinidad. Remember the ship is your hotel during

CARNIVAL

My brother Adolphus had invited me,
To Trinidad, an island in the Caribbean Sea
For Carnival in February an event most rare.
But alas! I was not there.

For plane tickets from the U.S. to Trinidad the agent said
Pay in 24 hrs. a sum of money that was over my head,
Was the only way to guarantee the fare.
But alas! I was not there.

To see mud on oiled bodies at last.
Old and young all add a special favor to Jvouvert mas.
Swaying, gyrating, dancing to Tassa drum without care.
But alas! I was not there.

Tapestry a release of human energy,
Music, colors, dance blending together without apology.
Peter Minshall and Callaloo Co. won band of the year.
But alas! I was not there.

When the big big truck went by,
With Masqueraders there arose a sigh,
For Machel Montano and Xtatix road march winner here.
But alas! I was not there.

Where calypso and soca star Crazy went from odd,
To being just plain crazy for God.
Proving music can be a form of praise everywhere.
But alas! I was not there.

When they mixed soca music with reggae.
Forming a very popular music in Jamaica called soggae.
Another sound evolved from calypso making a pair.
But alas! I was not there.

The calypso monarch, Gypsy, sang "Little Black Boy".
A social commentary not a musical toy.
Also Zola Pilgrim, female calypsonian, did appear.
But alas! I was not there.

The smell of Princess cooking fried fish and pelau,
Fried bakes, at Lord Kitchener's calypso Revue.
Hot & cold drinks, but fish broth is her specialty its clear.
But alas! I was not there.

See 75 yr. old Lord Kitchener's masterpiece Guitar Pan.
It proves the Grand master still can
Weave his genius for calypso and steel band.
But alas! I was not there.

But Panoramas steel bands are the best part
Sharpe, Samarro, Greenidge capturing many hearts.
In Tobago all-female Ban Fanatics made a good start.
But alas! I was not there.

To see carnival queens from Caribbean Classics,
Lost realms and Tribal Explosion did not panic,
Nor did Africa the Naked Truth and Forbidden Planet.
But alas! I was not there.

Also carnival kings Saragossa and Clash of Culture.
Dragon's Moko Jumbies will venture,
While dancing stilts making giant strides into the future.
But alas! I was not there.

To see the pretty women everywhere.
In elaborate costumes or almost bare,
All sizes and colors were exceedingly fair.
But alas! I was not there.

Skimpy costumes and great big masks,
But they only cover half she ass,
Giving heart attacks as she dances past.
But alas! I was not there.

She's showing all of her leg and most of her breast.
It makes you want to beg to see the rest.
Maybe it's for the best.
That alas! I was not there.

To see Carnival with my brother is my goal.
Queen's Park Savannah & Panorama a banner to hold.
Oh! To enjoy Carnival one can never be too old.
But alas! In August I will be there.

Check your list carefully, one of the few things you can't take through customs is

ANGER

Dictionary = a strong feeling of extreme annoyance,
Wrath, rage, displeasure, aggravation, just being mad.
If you use discernment you'll discover in a sense,
That the reality of anger is your own frustration,

At your inability to control someone else.
Knowing it is wrong to even try to control anyone
With a display of your inflated value of self.
It's impossible to change another person's opinion;

Through the use of angry words and threats of violence.
They only build a wall between you and the person
Or persons you are trying to influence.
Causing them to resist, moving in the opposite direction.

Many different kinds of anger are often displayed subtly.
The one we're most likely to encounter thus,
The most recognizable anger is directed outwardly
At others, at situations or events not related to us.

For example someone tearing up or trashing,
And canceling a magazine subscription,
Because they dislike the politics of a person appearing,
On the cover of this month's edition.

This we need to understand is activated
By the futility of anger over something that
We can not control or have regulated.
Resulting in uncontrolled useless action in fact.

Other types of anger are often directed inward,
Such as guilt which is anger at ourselves,
For doing something we consider wrong or untoward.
An after effect of sin as self condemnation rings its bells.

The peals of a guilty conscience will resound
So loud that no accuser will be needed
To shine the light until the deed is found.
Making you wish God's word you had heeded.

Then there is insecurity-anger at ourselves
For believing we are not good enough.
That our talents and abilities are like the elves,
Unseen and unappreciated by unbelievers this is rough.

Considering that with a little faith from us,
The Holy Spirit will magnify our talents
And abilities especially when working for Jesus.
Just make the effort and He will take care of the balance.

Now a poor self-Image is a destructive type of anger,
That may or may not be hard to detect.
When you lack self-esteem there is the danger,
That no one else will think your worthy of respect.

Some people with this problem stay in the shadows
Wasting time as they whimper and hide.
What they could have accomplished only God knows.
They were doomed to failure because they never tried.

Others pretend to be what they are not, but they hurt.
The bully, Casanova, hustler, Mc Daddy & entrepreneur.
The femme fatale, debutante, coquette, prostitute & flirt.
Who without God's help will be overwhelmed by failure.

Leading to depression= anger turned inward in a sense;
Difficult to detect and very painful to go through.
Only the awareness of God's loving presence
Will keep it from eventually destroying you.

Heed the words of Paul the Apostle, who warned us,
Not to allow the sun to set on our anger.
Let go of it quickly before it harms you, and trust
In the Lord to deliver you from false friends & strangers.

Now to start off tonight's game of twenty questions. Can anyone

Tell me

If con is the opposite of pro,
Is Congress the opposite of progress?
I really would like to know.

Why is lemonade made with artificial flavor,
And dishwashing liquid made with real lemons?

Why do people buy flowers for the dead
Who can neither see nor smell,
Whether they are in heaven or hell?

Tell me why vegetarians eat
Vegeburgers that look and taste like meat.
And consider it a treat.

Does anyone know why the man who invests
All your money is called a broker?

Why do they sterilize the needle
They use for lethal injections at executions?
It's too late to worry about infections.

Has anyone ever figured out why,
The sun lightens our hair
But darkens our skin whether dark or fair?

Explain the reason the time of day with
The slowest traffic is called the rush hour.

Why is it I've never seen the headline,
"Psychic wins the lottery the tenth time"?

Why do banks offer so many options,
Then charge you for too many transactions?

Why are living quarters called apartments,
When they are all stuck together?

Why do doctors call what they do practice?

Why don't sheep shrink when it rains?

Why isn't there mouse-flavored cat food?

Why is "abbreviated" such a long word?

I wonder, why women can't put on
Mascara with their mouths closed?

Why is it in court all the witnesses
Have to swear to tell the truth,
But the lawyers don't?

Tell me why they make the black box recorder
On airplanes out of indestructible
Material and not the rest of the plane?
To me this borders on the insane.

And if air travel is so safe today,
Why do they still call the airport the terminal?

Tell me why they serve good liquor on all
Airlines but good food on none of them?

Here in the south we have always wondered
Why Noah didn't swat those two mosquitoes.

Tell me why with all the hype about modern
Psychology mothers still say,
"This is going to hurt me more than it does you"?

This is a true story. Sometimes the truth seems like something from "The Twilight Zone;" as we travel along and watch a game of

PEPPER BALL

This is the tale of Mr. Viris Brown
A physically and mentally
Handicapped African-American
Male, in Lake Elsinore next to our town.

Two years ago he was sent by his mother
To the home of Miss Velma Jones,
Who had a heart condition to check on her.
He arrived only to discover

Her suffering from a heart attack
In need of a doctor or hospital.
Viris was afraid she was going to die.
So he dialed 911 and that's a fact.

When they didn't come right away, he became
So frustrated with the process he called
911 again and said if Miss Jones died,
He would kill himself or so they claim.

He said this believing it would bring
An ambulance and help, out faster.
When the operator told the dispatcher
He has a knife and not to pull his string.

A possible suicide attempt is no fun.
Better dispatch paramedics to help.
However sheriff dispatchers sent it out
As an assault with a deadly weapon.

One black whose name was Graves a deputy
Familiar with Brown who had made some
Previous 911 calls for assistance,
In the past when he was on duty.

Asked Brown how he was, if he'd taken his pills.
Said he was going to get cigarettes for him
He left brown who had been injured previously
Leaning on his quad cane for support, still

According to Mrs. Phillips his mother,
As soon as Graves left pepper balls started
Flying thirty six shots in all were fired.
Mother and sister had to seek cover.

The deputies shouted "drop the knife",
Which he did right after the third shot,
Then he fell or was knocked to the ground
Where he lay in pain and fears for his life.

He had been hit by twelve pepper balls,
Which cause not only bruises but second
Degree burns on contact along with an
Irritating powder, but worst of all,

Eight shots were fired after he was down.
As Brown lay defenseless he was then told
This time it was pepper balls the next time
Will be bullets by a sergeant with a frown.

An officer ground his foot into Brown's
Injured knee his screams were heard by neighbors,
Along with the laughter of other officers,
At Brown in pain from his leg to his crown.

He had been shot in the eye, arm and other
Parts of his body was coughing, choking
And bleeding surrounded by powder.
All of this was witnessed by his mother.

The paramedic said this was the worst case
He had ever seen, it would be a miracle
If he survived. Why this happened to
A disabled member of a minority race

Is what we need to find out and never
Let it happen again to anyone
Regardless of disability or race.
In Riverside or anywhere else ever.

Then to add insult to injury,
The district attorney not only filed
A misdemeanor charge, brandishing a knife
But added what amounted to perjury,

Two felony charges of assault
With a deadly weapon against Miss Jones,
The heart patient claiming he attacked and
Stabbed her. Making it seem like it's his fault.

Miss Jones told the prosecutor and the judge
That she had not been attacked or stabbed.
Mr. Brown was just trying to help her,
He didn't hurt anyone but they would not budge.

Not only did they refuse to drop the charges
At the hearing the deputies claimed
Viris Brown charged at them with the knife
Can a man using a quad cane charge?

Using this excuse the Judge sent him to jail.
Added two more felony counts on,
Raised the price from 50,000 dollars
To 100,000 dollars for bail.

While in jail he was denied access
To his medication for several weeks,
Thus causing the left side of his body
To go numb and other forms of distress.

Last year Brown was transferred to Patton state
Hospital. Declared mentally incompetent
By the court appointed physicians.
Then sent back to prison in apparent haste,

Without notifying his parents.
An obvious abuse of his and their
Civil rights by the justice system
In Riverside county. It doesn't make sense.

All Viris Brown did was ask for help.
What he got in return was pepper balled.
And a two year fight just to keep the law
From taking his tomorrows, he felt.

We all feel the handicapped man or wife
And the disabled whether mentally
Or physically, have a God given right
To have a harassment free decent life.

It is my job to guide you away from this travesty and
see that no one on this tour has any reason for

A LAMENT

In my travels I have seen cultures
Move from light to darkness without hope.
Dragged down to hell by humiliated
Souls bent under intolerable yokes.

Their days are filled with misery,
Distress for both husband and wife.
Nights flooded with tears and anguish.
I have seen many people
who are slaves of life.

I saw the marks of his chains in the sand,
The strong man marched shackled and subdued.
The faithful on their knees worship Idols
While by the priest they are used and abused.

I saw the trainee slave for the journeyman,
Employee slave for employer on and on it went.
Employer slaved for the soldier, who slaved
For the governor, who slaved for the President.

In the east the infant gets the milk
Of slavery from his mothers breast.
Children learn submission along with
The alphabet for them there is no rest.

Nor is there for women forced by
Custom and passivity to wear garments
Of restrictions and live lives accepting
Culturally forced reliance.

Where wives retire with tears
To men upon beds of obedience.
Forced by their own parents
Into legal compliance.

I saw slavery everywhere
Like a trail of ignorance.
People sacrificed their maidens and youth,
Calling her (God) what nonsense.

They burned Incense and poured wine
At her feet calling her King or Queen
Before kneeling and worshipping her,
Calling her the law, I wanted to scream.

They submitted to her will,
Fighting and dying for her sake.
Destroyed homes and institutions,
Called her patriotism! Will they ever awake?

Struggling and stealing they call
Her fraternity, what a mess.
A lifetime working for her,
The privileged call her happiness.

She is known by many names,
But she is void of nobility.
She has many appearances,
But there is only one reality.

Slavery is the one element
Or malignant cancerous virus,
In truth an everlasting plague.
That has been passed on by us.

In each and every generation
Unto his or her successor to save.
From city to country to nation,
No matter what flag they wave.

I beg and plead that we finally heed,
The Word crucified on Calvary.
For only through Jesus Christ,
Can we find the cure and true liberty.

Now we traverse the city's highways and byways
deep into the ghetto, where we will meet the

GHETTO BOY

Born in the ghetto one night was he;
Mother didn't remember how he came to be.
She was so high that even I could see
That her mind was floating free.

So into the system he was placed,
From one foster home to another he raced,
Trying to find a friendly face…
But always feeling out of place.

He went to school and came out a dunce;
A teacher tried to get through to him once.
He listened to peers and called the teacher a punk,
Thinking in the eyes of the girls he would be a hunk.

Never learned to read or much about math--
Anyone who made fun would suffer his wrath.
He did not want to study or learn to write.
He would rather go and pick a fight.

All he studied was his shoes and clothes.
The only thing learned was how to dress and pose.
He would do anything to be cool
In front of the women (what a fool).

He left school with no skills,
Only tagging walls and freeway signs for thrills.
He couldn't find much work or a steady job.
So he decided he would rob.

With money from a crap game won,
He got some weed and then a gun,
Smoked a joint to clear his head,
Entered the store and got shot instead.

He went to the hospital almost dead,
And awoke to find a Christian in the next bed
Who prayed to God for his survival,
Read to him about Christ from his bible…

Two weeks later taught him how to pray…
He got down on his knees that very day,
Praying to God to make things right.
He got the Spirit that same night.

That Sunday he accepted Jesus Christ,
Joined the church and vowed to fight
Satan and all of his devices
If he survived this crisis.

Since he was still under age,
Through Christ had gotten rid of all that rage,
The judge released him to the pastor,
Knowing he'd recover physically and spiritually.

Now he is painting commercial signs
(Instead of committing crimes)
Because a Christian decided to pray
And showed him Jesus is the way.

There comes a time, whether looking forward or back, that you realize you're on

Borrowed Time

It is time I would borrow
Since each year with more sorrow
I note with dismay
That my scalp of today
Will be forehead tomorrow

In spite of that even nature is celebrating our journey by throwing

Confetti

Autumn leaves floating
Upon the swirling breezes
Coloring the sky

One of the most gratifying aspects of this journey has been sharing it with

MY FRIEND

Norman Woods grew up in Los Angeles.
I grew up three thousand miles away.
When I first saw Norm in Detroit he was a Lion.
That's right, no I'm not lying.

Oh! How the crowd did roar,
When Norm made a catch and went on to score.
Too soon he had to end his football career.
But he did everything but disappear.

When he married the beautiful Carmelita.
No one could have been as intelligent or sweeter.
With her behind him he could boast,
Of three careers policeman, teacher and coach.

Also a husband, father and friend that's true,
To Diona, Ted, Ricky and Darcel too.
And he became a proud home owner
In a city in California called Pomona.

About that time I moved from N.Y. to L. A. then,
On to the city of Pomona where we met again.
Carmelita and Norm made us feel like family,
Betty, Tony, Neecy, Deborah, Jason and me.

For many years our families together we did raise.
For Norman & Carmelita we've nothing but praise.
In elementary, high school and college that's a fact,
He trained our children in sports, football and track.

As friends we spent birthdays & holidays together,
At children's meets, games in all kinds of weather.
Norm was an inspiration & role model you see,
Not only to the children but to the whole community.

We would get together for football on Monday night,
Or after watching a championship fight,
Sit around the pool, Norm was always Mr. Cool,
While watching Ricky and I play the fool.

Or sometimes trying to give advice to Ted ,
Whose ideas were always above everybody's head.
Then listening to Diona the queen,
Who accomplished anything she tried, it seemed.

Because of training Ricky who never had a plan,
Was good enough to be invited to be a L. A. Ram.
Even Darcel followed in his footsteps you see,
When she entered into the Police Academy.

Into each life comes some tragedy ,
For Norm a heart attack and by-pass surgery.
He never lost his spirit or pleasant personality,
As he worked toward a full recovery.

Still he took time to workout with me at his place.
Although I could never keep up with his pace.
Even after surgery he did more sets,
Of exercises and more weights than I could get.

Norm always faced responsibility unlike others.
Despite problems took care of Carmelita's mother.
By taking care of her the rest of her life,
He showed how much he cared for his wife.

Although Betty and I got divorced and moved away.
We both love Carmelita and Norm to this very day.
They never found fault or tried to place blame.
When we saw them they treated us just the same.

Accepted my wife Rean as she came on the scene,
With open arms, you know they were never mean.
We never forgot New Year's Eves spent together.
Just toasting, talking and enjoying one another.

Carmelita & family although you're hurting don't fret.
The end has not come, no not yet.
Look deep down inside and you will find,
A place in your heart where he will live for all time.

For your own safety, it always pays to keep your eyes and ears open and look

BEHIND THE MASK

Listen; can you hear what I'm not saying?
I tell everyone confidence is my name
That I don't need help from anyone else,
That's right they all know coolness is my game.

Don't be fooled by my face or my grace
Pretending is an art that's second nature
To me, I always give the impression
I'm unruffled and all is sunny and secure.

Hear what I'm not saying, don't believe me,
My surface may be smooth but it's a mask.
I wear a thousand masks that I'm afraid
To take off, what lies beneath? You may ask.

Behind various ever concealing masks
Impersonating life none of them are me.
Beneath lies no smugness, complacence or pride
Below dwells the real me adrift in a sea.

Of confusion, loneliness and fear
While I idly chatter in suave tones,
My routine surface talk filled with lies
To conceal pain that penetrates the bone.

I tell you what really amounts to nothing,
Saying everything except the truth
(Still crying out within me for release)
Buried since the early days of my youth.

Please don't be fooled by what I'm saying,
Listen carefully; hear what's not said,
What I'd like to be able to discuss,
Need to but can't get out of my head.

My survival depends on your ear,
Only you can pull me back into life
Each time your kind, gentle or encouraging
Trying to relieve my stress and strife.

When I realized you really cared
My troubled heart began to grow wings,
Very small wings, feeble wings, but wings
You need to know this among other things.

With your sensitivity, sympathy
And the power of understanding
You'll be able to breathe life into me
Little by little without grand standing.

I want you to know how important
You are. How you can be a creator
Of the special person that will be me,
If you choose to be my benefactor.

Do not pass me by. It won't be easy,
My long conviction of worthlessness
Has built many high strong walls that form
What amounts to a veritable fortress.

The nearer you approach the worse I get
May even strike out. I fight against
The very thing I cry out and sigh for
Vanquished by your sight and unique scent.

I have been told love is stronger than
Any walls, in this lay my only hope,
My only hope. Who am I you may wonder,
Look past the mask, smoke, habit or dope.

I am someone you know so very well
A hurting member of your family,
The person sitting here beside you,
Every she or he you meet really

Don't believe what you see get behind
The mask, glimpse the individual the real
Me. Take time to recognize my true self
At the very least grant my appeal.

Because when you care you love and share.

No matter what season, city or country, whether you travel a little or a lot it's

AT YOUR OWN RISK

Most think having this product makes them happy
And gives them the time they will need to succeed.
Believing they have the power to fulfill dreams,
Able to acquire everything they need.

They don't seem to realize the use of this product,
May cause apathy and laziness leading to,
A false sense of security and empowerment,
Combined with superficial values you will rue.

Their self centered manipulative behavior,
In the absence of individuality
Coupled with selfish greed and gluttony will bring
To the ignorant a change of Identity.

The accompanying lack of spirituality,
Leaves one open to possible participation,
In environmental destruction, war, murder,
Impoverishment for others and racial tension.

Continuous and excessive use could initiate
A permanent state of indifference to others.
The World and the welfare of those around you.
Forgetting they are still your sisters and brothers.

Use sparingly at your own risk follow the rules
This product is known as Satan's number one tool.
In fact it is the root of all evil even
The Bible says love of this makes one cruel.

Yes I am talking about money, gold and wealth,
Over indulgence may cause an exaggerated
Sense of pride if not tempered with Christ's love.
So be careful, don't abuse, it is overrated

Use at your own risk.

Whether you just joined the tour or were here from the start, I guarantee you will go home satisfied with your travel

EXPERIENCE

After awhile you learn the subtle difference,
Between holding a hand and chaining a soul.
There can be a very dire consequence,
To doing everything you want or are told.

Love doesn't necessarily mean leaning,
And company doesn't mean security.
You must look for a deeper meaning,
Before you sacrifice your purity.

Begin to learn that kisses are not contracts,
And that presents are not promises.
Or you will look at life through cataracts,
While depending on doubting Thomas's.

You can begin to accept your defeats,
With your head held up and your eyes open,
Learning what you should not repeat,
In order to face the world less often.

With the grace of a woman,
Not the grief of a child.
With the esteem of a worthy man,
Not the temper of a boy gone wild.

Plan to build all your roads on today,
Because tomorrow's ground is too uncertain.
Do what you can with what you have is the way,
To accomplish your goals and win again.

Now from experience you will learn,
That even sunshine burns if you get too much.
So don't fret about how much you earn.
Just be sure with God you keep in touch.

So plant your own garden,
And decorate your own soul.
Your sins He will surely pardon,
Because for us Christ's life was sold.

Look at your instruction sheet. Any question on it has been answered every day for the last month. If at the conclusion of the orientation meeting your question is on the sheet

Don't Ask

Don't ask me now to venerate
A man who's so degenerate
Always arrives an hour late
He slobbers on his dinner plate
And nods asleep at ten or eight

Excuse me for a moment while I try to put an end to this

Serenade

A tomcat meows
Out of the dark come the shoes
And the flower pot

The company would like to remind you we are not as young as we used to be, so take the necessary precautions. In our age group it can be dangerous trying to be

COOL

There is the possibility
That you thought you were cool
Just because you went to grammar school,
Was a sign that humility
And the sense of reality,

Both had been missing for sometime.
Bragging about the two welfare
Checks that you receive not aware,
Of it being a major crime,
Leading to more than a small fine.

Now we all have to pay our dues,
I know! I know you think its cool,
Double dipping on welfare. You fool!
If you don't listen to my news,
You'll catch the 10-year jailhouse blues.

I'm cool she told mother Maddy,
I care for my child like a hen,
Collect child support from two men;
Neither one's the baby's daddy,
Picked because they drove a Caddy.

Your smokes are not menthol or kools.
Say what! Snorting is not doing any harm,
What about those tracks on your arm,
You must be crazy or a fool,
Don't you know you're the Devil's tool?

You don't have anything to lose?
What about body soul and mind?
Memories all that's left behind.
Its time to use some bible clues
And put on your walking shoes.

Listen to truth in Bible found
Instead of shootin and noddin,
Be wise and ask for God's pardon.
Only Christ can turn you around,
And put you back on solid ground.

Go to church and then to school,
Repent before it's too late,
For His grace you don't have to wait,
Follow God's commands and golden rule,
Before you can claim to be cool.

Lay back close your eyes and relax we want
you to be comfortable as we share

THE VISION

This is the vision that came to me.
One night I was on my knees
Praying God would let me know
What it would take for Him to be pleased.

When suddenly I was lifted up high,
Carried to a place over looking a path
Next to a field where a body of believers
Were discussing how to avoid God's wrath.

We will enter into a covenant,
With God, the church and the world in happiness.
Because by the marvelous light of the word
We have been called out of darkness.

To develop a true Christian community
Where every man, woman, boy and girl
Will share Christ word and teaching
With each other and with the world.

We have been called to transform
The world, a dual calling,
First by example being Christ like
Teaching others how to avoid falling.

Second by obeying the Commandments,
With the Holy Spirits guidance doing His will.
Inviting all persons to have a personal relationship
With God through faith in Jesus, who will fill,

Their hearts with the power of the Holy Spirit
To exist in unity where His love prevails,
Bear witness to God's name through Jesus
Doing all we can to bring glory to God.

Our mission to bring salvation to mankind.
I continued to watch as they started
Down the divine path and were joined
By people of all races, never again to be parted.

The congregation grew as they traveled
From town, to city, to country, to continent,
Destined to finally cover the world.
So that even God would be content.

Suddenly I was back on my knees,
Wondering where the vision went.
I could almost feel the ground vibrate,
From marching feet, I knew it was heaven sent.

Before we leave this romantic spot those of you who are alone I suggest you talk to your

Valentine by Phone

When I hear you on the phone,
Your voice turns me on with a mellow tone.
When I see you on the street,
My whole body gets weak.

My heart has been waiting like a dove,
While my soul has been anticipating your love,
I've just been barely alive,
While my arms have been waiting for you to arrive.

From the time I awake,
I imagine the good love we will make.
Just imagine how it's going to feel,
When we hug and kiss I'll know it's real.

I don't care how long it takes you see,
I know you are the woman for me.
We cannot deny ourselves the chance
Of being a part of the right romance.

Fellow travelers we've come a long way to hear the

Truth Not Silence

Though you put your finger to your lip
Counseling first silence and then threatening,
Still I will not be silent.
I will not pick my words.
Will I speak from the depths of my heart?
Yes, even if forewarned you are violent.

In this day and age an enlightened man
May speak without endangering his freedom.
In times past the truth was kept mute.
Only the poet dared to shatter the silence.
This poets words will flow like a flood,
A testimony to verify the truth.

Although some may doubt or even deny,
I know that truth is the tongue of God
And has never been voiceless.
God is truth and love together.
Eternity will not change them.
Neither comes before the other nor is less.

God's justice is the truth.
His mercy all the attributes of God.
My lamentations break through,
My cheeks are wet with tears.
These eyes cups that overflow
To drench the altars of these two.

On one altar Virtue lies in dismay
Who though not rich, was proud
Now sleeps overwhelmed by vanity.
On the other altar illustrious Liberty
Who never in life feared death,
Now smothered by adversity.

Once upon a time growing old in fortunes arms
Was an affront contrived by the passing years.
To wile away the time in idleness,
Was alien to our youth, in the past
They didn't count years only how they lived them,
Each hour marked with restlessness.

Eagerly striving after valiant deeds,
Flourishing Virtue was mistress then
Ruling the people of that age.
Though not eloquent, resounded with victories.
Open your eyes embrace the truth.
Return to when Liberty was the rage.

One thing about being on a long journey it gives us a legitimate excuse not to keep

A Commitment

I love a church that worships,
    The way that Jesus taught.
Having service on every Sabbath,
    With the Spirit as we aught.

I go there on Sabbath morning,
    Because I know it's right.
But, to go there on Wednesday,
    Has always been a fight.

I love to sing the songs of praise'
    Such worship must be right.
So I sing on Sabbath morning,
    But not on Wednesday night.

I love to hear the gospel preached,
    It gives me such delight.
So I listen every Sabbath morning,
    But not on Wednesday night.

Bless the pastors message Lord,
Oh Spirit! Fill him with your power and might.
To put the sinner in his place,
For I wont be there Wednesday night

I 'll go through rain or sleet or storm,
Do anything that's right.
To be at church on Sabbath morn,
But not on Wednesday night.

I know I'm weak and need more strength,
To keep me in the Church.
Every Sabbath morning I sit on the front bench.
But on Wednesday night in that seat I'll not perch.

Someday the Lord will surely come.
I hope I'll be doing right
So I pray He comes on Sabbath morning,
And not on Wednesday night.

Even though there seems to be plenty of time, be on the safe side

DON'T WAIT

Time waits for no one.
It doesn't matter if you've just begun
Or if you think that you're done.
Time passes for everyone.

The evidence is there to see--
Cataracts for you, arthritis for me...
None of us are wrinkle free.
Time will take the mind on a forgetful spree.

Time like God is invisible for all intents.
When accused like Christ is silent,
Although weightless, will cause the back to be bent.
Searched for, one wonders where it went.

You can feel its burden on your shoulders,
Especially as you grow older.
Then it hits you like a boulder.
There is never enough and no one can hold her.

So spread Christ's word now before it's too late,
Because time doesn't stop while we deliberate.
We know only God can make it wait
While we prepare our souls for that final date.

We don't want to remember a life that was a waste.
Before the love of Christ, we could taste.
With time passing like the wind in haste
Before we can get the victory over sin.

After you disembark be sure to take a picture of the

Night Lights

Bring true joy
Light up darkened sky
Cruise blue seas

I am happy to say that after checking in we still have time for

Reflections

My face and the sun
Floating next to a lily
Dancing in ripples

Ladies and Gentlemen: I would like to thank you for allowing me to be your guide on this "Journey Through the Mind of a Poet." With your cooperation we will board our flight home in

JUST AN HOUR

Just an hour devoted to the pursuit of beauty
And love is worth a century of glory,
Given by the frightened and weak as a duty
To the Strong is the gist of this story.

For that hour man absorbs the essence of truth.
While for the next century truth sleeps
Like a hibernating bear without a tooth,
Man in fear utters not a cry or peep.

In that hour the soul sees for itself,
The natural law of God, a real find.
For a century man imprisons himself
Behind the laws and customs of mankind.

One hour lamenting those that are shackled
With the irons and burdens of oppression,
Is like a century filled with war, debacle,
Hunger, disease and worldwide destruction.

One hour devoted to mourning the history
Of the stolen equality of the weak.
Is nobler than a century
Filled with greed and usurpation of the meek.

That hour was the inspiration
Of the Songs of Solomon,
That century was the blind power of destruction
Of the people and temple of Jerusalem.

That hour was the glorious birth
Of the sermon on the mountain.
That century forgot Christ came to earth,
Moses on Sinai, Golgotha and Allah that's certain.

It is at that hour when the heart
Is purified by the flaming arrow of sorrow
Illuminated in full not just a part,
By the torch of love today and tomorrow.

While in this century the desire
For truth is buried in the bosom of the earth,
Where it is smothered like dirt on a fire,
Thus hiding its value or worth.

This is the hour of contemplation
In which the root must flourish.
For a century the rich indulge in self gratification,
At the expense of the earth, river and forest.

At last the hour of meditation,
Not only throughout the neighborhood
But throughout the nation,
To usher in a new era of good.

This hour portrayed on stages for ages,
By our elders and our peers,
Recorded on earth for centuries by sages
And lived in bewildering strangeness for years.

Although sung as a hymn for days,
Is exalted for only an hour.
But that hour is treasured in many ways
By eternity as a jewel of infinite power.

While we are waiting here is a point to ponder, (who can you trust) pick up your earphones and listen to

The Witness

Three Pastors met and agreed to tell
one another a very pressing problem
A secret which surely must be kept
Between the three until they solve them

The first Pastor said please pray for me
You see stealing money is my thing
This has gotten to be a criminal offense
I even steal from the church offering

The second Pastor said I must confess
A desire for women is my addiction
To go to bed with every woman I see
Has become my fulltime affliction

In fact I've slept with most of our Church
Female members single or married
Old and young so bold that I'm afraid
I'll be caught and to the grave be carried

Turning to the third Pastor he was shocked
To see him crying as he took a tissue
As they made an effort to calm him
Still crying he said you don't know my issue

When they asked the Pastor to continue
He cried you see gossiping is my sin
With tears still running down his cheeks
Declared there is no way for us to win

When we finally take our leave of this place
Everybody will hear everything
That the two of you have just told me
Pray for me you know I have to sing.

Just as we promised for your final leg here is your

Window Seat

Looking down
At the clouds floating
On blue skies

Going through customs I hear a voice calling my name I look around in

Recognition

In the check-out line
A worn face ahead of me
Turns tentatively

Finally you recognize the fact that you made it
through customs makes this trip a

Success

Have you ever wondered what it really is?
Research shows that the most common definition
Is the attainment of wealth, favor, fame and power.
Or any one, depending on individual perception.

The dictionary says it is the satisfactory
Completion of something, the favorable
Outcome of an attempt or one that succeeds.
I'd like to put another version on the table.

For me being successful is knowing
The difference between what is important
And what is not. To personally maintain
A healthy body and mind still rational and vibrant

To be free from internal and external clutter.
Have the time and energy to sustain
A resonant connection to those I love.
To live life without a reason to complain.

To have the respect of children, family, friends,
Peers and the community. But most of all,
To continue to have opportunities to
Develop my talents and skills and not fall

Under the influence of Satan and his minions.
And still have a viable relationship with God.
I hope Each one of you will enjoy success.
Whatever the definition as you walk with God.

Now that you're back I must congratulate you on your safe return to your:

LIFE

>What is life? Can anyone tell me?
>Where are the yesteryears I lived?
>My times controlled by circumstance,
>The hours, Alzheimer's hides you see.
>
>What I know, I know not how but fear
>My health and years have fled.
>Living attends to failures and victories,
>Although calamities still pursue me here.
>
>Yesterday was, tomorrow has not come,
>Today goes on without a pause
>Or even a reasonable cause,
>Their value by age outdone.
>
>Vanquished(I was, will be and am
>In today, tomorrow and yesterday
>conjoined, from diapers to the shroud
>I travel still on this lonely road)
>By the grave and Uncle Sam.

I almost forgot, before you fade from view
I'd like to say :
Thank You

It is rare to find a person,
Who accepts you for what you are,
And without reservation,
Compared to others you area star.

Who also makes you feel good
About being yourself,
In spite of knowing you could,
Have left me on the shelf.

I thank you for helping me to find,
The best part of who I am too,
And I thank you for being kind,
Enough to let me share it with you.

I hereby bestow upon you, my heart.
With the hope you will accept,
All of me, each and every part,
To do with as you will except reject.

Ladies and Gentlemen we have a special guest joining us for our farewell party. I have the honor to introduce

The Sunshine Man

Arrived at the hotel in an electric truck
Sporting many kinds of signs in reality
Go vegan was the one that really stuck
Out along with down with the death penalty

The sun reflected on the many buttons bound
To the tie around his neck that shone like beacons
Indoors words light up the stage as he expounds
On the virtues of N.V.C….the pros and cons

This facilitator of our non-violent
Compassionate Communication Practice Group
From a "language of Life as a secret agent"
By Marshall Rosenberg… author and guru

To foster recognition of universal needs
Ours and concern for the well-being of others
Teaches that memnoons are connected to deeds
That lead to treating all as sisters and brothers

Based on a long list of emotions that we might
Experience when our needs are being met
If they were not realized may lead to a fight
Using emotions listed in the negative set

Giving examples of how empathy can turn
A bad situation around when applied
Using the N.V.C. rules he wanted us to learn
The sunshine man encouraged us when we tried

On the other side we endeavored to convince
Him to add God to his belief in N.V.C.
Even using logic it will always make sense
Not only to him but also to you and me

Without God people will forget what was said
Soon no one will remember anything he did
Involve God all will recall the truth he read
Praise for gifts, talents and works won't be hid

But the most important thing people will never
Forget what emotions were evoked and how
He made them feel, lives were changed forever
For this thank the sunshine man here and now

It has been a pleasure being your guide on this "Journey Through the Mind of a Poet". I'll wave goodbye as you take those last

A Half a Dozen Steps

A half a dozen steps taken carefully
Will insure a world of boundless joy
If we take these steps seriously
As we walk the path of life together

Each step has its own value which will accrue
An abundant yield in most situations
These values are worthwhile and transcend
Nationalities, cultures and religions
When we accept them for what they are worth

Notice when written as a formula
Loyalty + compassion = fairness
This rule can be applied by young and old
To relieve others of unneeded stress

Trustworthiness + respect = responsibility
It is important to remember that
With power comes accountability
To be successful controlling this power
Be guided by adequate definitions

Loyalty is a tie that will bind
To keep one faithful to a cause or person
Unswerving allegiance or fidelity
To a duty bordering on piety

Compassion is a sympathetic
Consciousness of others distress
With a desire to alleviate the stress
Despite difficulty or adversity
Bearing trials calmly without complaint

Fairness is just and equitable treatment
Marked by impartiality and honesty
Free from self-interest or prejudice
Values that have no boundaries compliment

Trustworthiness is being dependable
And truthful while avoiding actions
That are detrimental to anyone else
Or favoring any other factions
One who will always keep his word

Respect is recognizing that everyone
Is worthy of esteem or consideration
Being open minded when you take
Into account another's qualifications

Responsibility is the state of being
Morally, legally and mentally
Accountable for all your own actions
Choosing to accept your obligation
To step into a world without boundaries

Walking along the path with these values
In your heart and with Christ at your side
You will realize that there are no boundaries
When you decide with God to abide

Post script

MENTOR

Mentor how did this come to be?
You are the teacher-advisor
Although I'm the oldest, hear me,
You seem to be much the wiser.

Your control so strong that nothing
Can disturb your peace of mind.
When you talk of life there's something
In it for each of us to find,

The health, happiness, and the love
That we seek with prosperity,
For every person you know above
Or below becomes a reality.

Making all your friends really feel
That there is something in them too;
When you make the sunny side real,
And your optimism comes true.

Thinking only the very best
Enthusiastic success,
Your own no more than all the rest,
You work and expect nothing less.

Easily forget the mistakes
Of the past, press on to greater,
Achievements where our future stakes,
Are always a little better.

Mentor so cheerful and wise,
Spending time on self improvement,
Leaves him no time to criticize,
Others, a trait that's heaven sent.

Who is willing to share his time,
Labor and knowledge with anyone.
Will fight anything he thinks is a crime.
Spirituality he hides from everyone.

Most people would laugh if you say
This rebel poet and activist,
Was anything like Christ, no way!
But I believe he's passed the test.

Just to be too large for worry,
To be too noble for anger,
And too strong for fear I'm sorry
To say is being Christ-like brother.

While being too happy to permit
Even the presence of trouble,
Don't question it-just accept it.
And please do not bust the bubble.

You see God made him too just like
He made you and I don't ask why,
He can inspire with a mic.
Just pray for the courage to try.

This poem is dedicated to:
My friend, fellow poet, writer,
And master of the spoken word
My mentor, Mr. Stephen Roper.

www.ingramcontent.com/pod-product-compliance
Lightning Source LLC
Chambersburg PA
CBHW032123090426
42743CB00007B/445